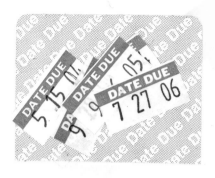

CORVETTE

THE AMERICAN SPORTS CAR

by
SHIRLEY HAINES
and
HARRY HAINES

THE ROURKE CORPORATION, INC.
Vero Beach, FL 32964

s and publisher wish to thank Chevrolet Motor Car
r invaluable assistance in compiling the technical
n for this book. Special thanks are due Ralph
d Mark Broderick for locating the photographs that
were obtained from Chevrolet. Special appreciation is owed to
David and Carol Burroughs of Bloomington Gold for the
photograph and certificate on page 20, and Lisa Leathery for
photographs of Corvettes at Carlisle on pages 21 and 26.
Kathleen Hunt at Callaway Cars provided photographs from
the following: Twin Turbo Callaway on page 4 by Jesse
Alexander, Sledgehammer on page 27 by D. Randy Riggs.

Special recognition is owed to Lee Buttram of Midway
Chevrolet (the Corvette dealer in Canyon, Texas) for his
continuous help, guidance and encouragement. Lee is the
consummate Corvette expert; the fact that he loves to talk
about the cars really helped this book.

Library of Congress Cataloging-in-Publication Data

Haines, Shirley, 1935-
      Corvette: the American sports car / by Shirley and Harry Haines.
        p. cm. – (Car classics)
      Summary: Gives a brief history of the Corvette automobile and
describes its special features and some classic models.
      Includes index.
      ISBN 0-86593-253-0
      1. Corvette automobile – Juvenile literature. [1. Corvette
automobile.] I. Haines, Harry, 1932-   . II. Title. III. Series: Car classics
(Vero Beach, Fla.)
    TL215.C6H35 1993
    629.222'2 – dc20   93-18066
                                                   CIP
                                                     AC

CONTENTS

CHAPTER 1

CORVETTE: *THE* AMERICAN SPORTS CAR

Corvette is America's only true sports car. It is as much a part of America as baseball or apple pie. When you read about this unusual piece of America's automobile history, the words *legend* and *legendary* are often used. The dictionary defines legendary as, "famous, often talked about." It might help the definition to include the words "… as in Corvette."

Most people remember their first ride in a Corvette. Whether it was a '57 Fuelie, a mid-'60s Sting Ray, a '70s "Coke bottle shaped" Mako Shark, or even today's ZR-1, the experience was unforgettable. The memory probably includes a feeling of pressure as the acceleration pushed you back against the seat.

In its early years the Corvette almost fizzled, and there was much talk about stopping production. It was made of plastic, seated only two, seemed impractical. Who would buy this car when, for less money, you could get a sedan that was made of metal and carried two or three times as many people in greater comfort? The answer, some 40 years later, was over 1 million customers. Obviously, some people want a car that is fast, sexy – more than just *ordinary* transportation. Today Chevrolet will sell you a street-legal, emissions-certified Corvette that'll do 170 mph plus. It's still made of plastic, seats only two, but it is now a world-class sports car that is truly *extraordinary* transportation.

A 190 mph Callaway Twin Turbo Corvette. Performance included 0-60 mph in 4.4 seconds, and the standing quarter-mile in 12.7 seconds at 113 mph. Read more about these "aftermarket" cars in Chapter 12.

A historic photograph: The 1,000,000th Corvette, July 2, 1992, with the only two men who served as "chief engineer" in the car's 40-year history, Zora Arkus-Duntov (left) and Dave McLellan.

On the pages that follow in this book are some of the most significant performance automobiles ever made in the world. They are all made in America. In fact, you could say Corvette is the "All-American" sports car.

CHAPTER 2

THE FIRST CORVETTE: 1953

In January, 1953, when Dwight Eisenhower was about to be inaugurated as the 34th president, General Motors opened its Motorama car show at the Waldorf Astoria hotel in New York City. Four million people visited the display and saw a small, two-seater, all-white, concept car rotating under the hot glare of spotlights. An attractive young woman gave a sales pitch while other women handed out brochures about the new car. It was named after a swift class of naval vessels called "Corvette."

Public response to the "dream car" was so strong that Harley Earle, GM's chief designer, urged immediate production. If only 1 percent of those people bought a Corvette, it would account for over 40,000 sales per year. Time was short to convert a concept car into a production model, so off-the-shelf parts had to be utilized as much as possible.

The beginning of the Corvette legend was the 1953 model. Corvette has grown to become the "flagship car" for the Chevrolet Division of General Motors. The head of Chevrolet now says, "There is a little Corvette in every car we build."

Model	1953
Period of production	June-December, 1953
Engine	Blue Flame Six, 235ci
Horsepower	150
Transmission	Powerglide 2-speed automatic
Maximum speed	105 mph
Acceleration 0-60 mph	11.5 seconds
Units produced	300 convertibles
Price	$3,498

Harley J. Earle was vice president of General Motors in charge of design during the '30s, '40s and '50s. He was the most famous car designer in the world when he introduced the Corvette in 1953.

The 1953 Corvette had no side windows nor outside door handles. It was regarded as a complete failure in terms of sales. Of the 300 that were made, 225 are accounted for today and have become valuable collector cars.

A standard Chevy sedan frame was shortened by 13 inches and fitted with an in-line 6-cylinder engine with 2-speed Powerglide automatic transmission. The engine was named "Blue Flame Six" and given triple carburetors. The 150 hp Six was far from a tire burner. It took 11.5 seconds to go from 0-60 mph.

The first Corvette rolled out of a makeshift production line in Flint, Michigan, on June 30, 1953. Only 300 cars were produced that year. All were white, with red interiors, and had black convertible tops.

CHAPTER 3

FASTER AND FASTER: 1954-62

A " '57 Fuelie," one of the most famous Corvettes ever made. It had fuel injection with a 4-speed Borg-Warner manual shift. Even in Turin, Italy, no one had fuel injection in 1957.

With high hopes for big sales, Corvette production was moved to GM's St. Louis plant in December, 1953. The plant was designed to build 10,000 Corvettes annually. However, only 3,640 cars were built in 1954 and of those, 1,100 remained unsold at the end of the model year. Something was clearly wrong, and the handwriting on the wall said that Corvette wasn't going to be around very long unless it was fixed quickly.

The fixer had an unusual name: Zora Arkus-Duntov. He is now referred to as the "Father of the Corvette." Duntov was both an experienced Chevrolet engineer and a racing enthusiast. History tells us he was the right man at the right place and the right time.

Duntov's first move was to change the old Blue Flame Six to Chevy's advanced small-block V-8. In his 1955 models, the 0-60 mph time dipped below nine seconds, and a quarter-mile was run in 17.2 seconds at 81.5 mph. In 1956 came roll-up windows, a sleek new body, and another increase in power. Corvette entered the record books by establishing a Daytona production-

CORVETTE

Zora Arkus-Duntov, the man now regarded as "Mr. Corvette." He was born in Russia but came to America in December, 1940. After joining the Corvette program in 1956, he was responsible for such advanced additions as fuel injection, disc brakes, independent rear suspension and limited slip differentials. Duntov was a two-time winner at LeMans and set a Pike's Peak stock car record that stood for 13 years.

class speed record of 150.5 mph. The company was starting to have second thoughts about stopping production.

If '55 and '56 models were noteworthy improvements, the '57 Corvette, with fuel-injection and 4-speed manual transmission, was an American automotive milestone. *Motor Trend Magazine* called it the " '57 Fuelie with eyeball-flattening acceleration." The car's 0-60 mph time was an amazing 7.2 seconds. Sales jumped to 6,339 units.

The models 1953 through 1962 are now called the "Classic Corvettes." Power increased every year and sales followed. Many call the '62 model the "best of the first generation 'Vettes."

Model 1962

Engine	327ci V-8 fuel-injected
Horsepower	360
Gearbox	Powerglide 2-speed automatic 3- or 4-speed manual
Acceleration 0-60 mph	5.9 seconds
Standing quarter-mile	14.9 seconds @ 102.5 mph
Units produced	14,531 convertibles

The 1962 model marked the end of the so-called "Classic Corvettes." It was the final year of exposed headlights, solid rear axle, conventional trunk and power top.

CHAPTER 4

STING RAY: 1963-67

In 1993 a national contest offered as its grand prize a choice between a brand new 1993 Corvette or a fully restored 30-year-old 1963 Corvette. The winner took the '63 model. Amazing? Not really, because the '63 was worth more than the new one. In fact, the "mid-year" Corvettes (models 1963 through 1967) have become the most collectible, and therefore the most expensive, of the series.

Even in 1963 Chevrolet knew it had a winner. The styling by Bill Mitchell was classic and still turns heads

In 1963, for the first time, Corvette was available as both a convertible and a coupe.

Model 1967	
Engine	Big-block V-8, 427ci
Horsepower	435 hp (some as high as 500)
Gearbox	Powerglide 2-speed automatic 3- or 4-speed manual
Maximum speed	135 mph
Acceleration 0-60 mph	5.6 seconds
Standing quarter-mile	13.4 seconds @105 mph
Units produced	22,940

today. For the first time Corvette came in two models, a convertible *and* a fastback coupe. Power steering, power brakes, aluminum knock-off wheels and air conditioning were available as options. The new suspension transformed the car's handling to a world-class level. A '63 tested by *Motor Trend* did 0-60 in 5.8 seconds. Customers had to wait months for delivery, as sales went through the roof. The Corvette factory added a second shift and produced 10,594 coupes and 10,919 convertibles – a new record of 21,513 cars for a model year.

In 1964 Chevrolet didn't mess with a great car. But 1965 brought big news under the hood as the first mega-motor big-block became available. It was a 396ci monster that produced 425 hp and 415 pound feet (lb-ft) of torque. In 1966 the big-block's displacement climbed to 427 cubic inches. *Motor Trend* described their test of a 390 hp version as follows: "In the relatively light, front-end heavy Corvette, this (power) tends to pave the highway with your rear-tire treads."

Many Corvette buffs think the '67 Sting Ray is the car to buy. As the last of the so-called "mid-year" 'Vettes, it is also the most refined.

One of the most distinctive styling features of the 1963 Corvette was the split rear window.

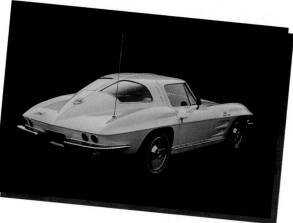

The 1967 Corvette has been called "the best Sting Ray ever." It was the last of the body styles now known as the "mid-year" models.

; 11

THE MAKO SHARK: 1968-82

First, let's settle the confusion about "Sting Ray" vs. "Stingray" and the years they were used. The models 1963 through 1967 used the two-word name, Sting Ray. The models 1969 through 1976 used a one-word designation, Stingray. And no, there was no "sting" of any kind used with the 1968 model.

At their 1965 car show, General Motors introduced a concept car called the "Mako Shark." It was later adapted and became the '68 Corvette. The new car's most celebrated styling feature was the ballooning fender treatment. Big wide fenders gave the car a Coke bottle shape. Automobile magazines disliked it and called it excessive and cumbersome. Still, the public loved it, and sales reached a record 23,562. Convertibles outsold coupes by 2-to-1.

A 1971 Corvette LT-1, "the last of the fast ones." This was the car that marked the end of the screaming big-block engines. Emission standards, catalytic converters and fuel economy became the buzzwords of the car industry.

In the period that followed, changes in appearance were minimal. The changes were in performance, and the 1970s became years of diminishing results. Big-block engines disappeared and horsepower fell to 165 at the darkest of times. Mako Shark styling aged well and easily accepted new demands for energy-absorbing bumpers. The convertible disappeared, the victim of low sales resulting from fears about safety standards.

The two men who had had greatest impact on Corvette retired from Chevrolet, chief engineer Zora Arkus-Duntov and chief stylist William Mitchell. They turned their car over to engineer Dave McLellan and stylist Jerry Palmer.

A 1982 model, the final and most refined version of the Mako Shark (Coke bottle shaped) Corvettes. From 1968 to 1982, 517,454 cars were built along these same dynamic lines.

Model	1977
Engine	V-8, 350ci
Horsepower	180 hp (some as high as 210)
Gearbox	4-speed manual or Hydra-Matic automatic
Maximum speed	120 mph
Acceleration 0-60 mph	8.9 seconds
Units produced	49,213 coupes

CHAPTER 6

NEW TREND 'VETTES: 1984 TO TODAY

There was no '83 model Corvette.

In March, 1983, Chevrolet introduced the all-new, 1984 Corvette. It was a complete redesign in every aspect. Handling considerations dominated, and the result was praised in magazines as the world's best-cornering automobile. The new car was lighter, roomier, quicker and more economical with fuel. Everyone thought the '84 model was a better looker. The public loved it, and 51,547 cars were produced, the second highest number in Corvette history.

Model	1984
Engine	V-8, 350ci
Horsepower	205 hp
Gearbox	4-speed manual or 4-speed automatic
Maximum speed	144 mph
Acceleration 0-60 mph	7.0 seconds
Standing quarter-mile	15.42 seconds @ 87.5 mph
Units produced	51,547 coupes
Base price	$21,800

The all-new 1984 Corvette. David McLellan, the car's principal engineer, was quoted as saying, "Acceleration, speed and braking performance are three of our primary concerns – not merely the ultimates of these capabilities, but how each interacts to create the total car." With this model, the automotive press began calling Corvette "the King of the Hill," a term still frequently used today.

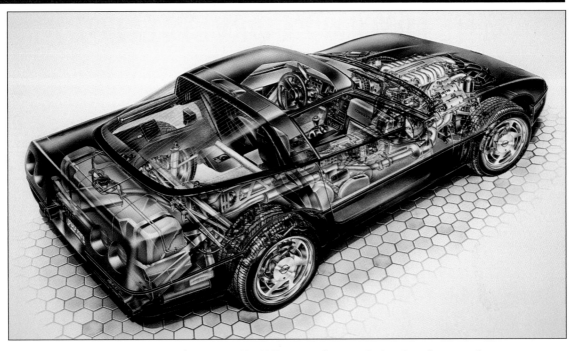

The ZR-1 Corvette appeared in 1990. After two decades of emphasis on natural resource conservation, it was incredible that Chevrolet could produce a fully licensed and street-legal 170-mph plus Corvette.

In '85, tuned-port injection boosted power to 230 hp. ABS (anti-lock brake system) was added in '86 and the convertible returned. Power increased again in '87 and the Callaway Twin Turbo package became a factory-ordered option. The Callaway option for '88 increased in power and price, to 382 hp and $26,345. An optional 6-speed manual shift with 4-gear override was added to the '89 'Vette.

The long-awaited ZR-1 became available with the 1990 models. It was a $27,016 option on top of the standard $31,979, a total of $58,995. Demand was so great dealers were charging up to $25,000 over sticker price. *Motor Trend's* test showed a 0-60 time of 4.8 seconds, a quarter-mile in 13.13 seconds at 110 mph, and a top speed of 177 mph. The ZR-1 proved that America could build a high-tech, 4-cam V-8 that performed with the best in the world.

CHAPTER 7

THE 1,000,000ᵀᴴ CORVETTE: 1992

The 1,000,000th Corvette, photographed with a 1953 model outside the Corvette plant in Bowling Green, Kentucky. This historic picture was made on July 2, 1992. Both cars are all-white with a red interior.

The first production Corvette rolled off a makeshift assembly line in Flint, Michigan, on June 30, 1953. The 1,000,000th unit, a 1992 convertible, was built at the Corvette Assembly Plant in Bowling Green, Kentucky, on July 2, 1992. Only three GM plants have ever built Corvettes – the 1953 Corvette at Flint, 1954 through 1981 models at St. Louis, and 1981 through present models at Bowling Green.

CORVETTE

David McLellan is only the second man in history to serve as chief engineer of the Chevrolet Corvette, the other being Zora Arkus-Duntov. During his 18-year tenure, McLellan developed the all-new 1984 model and the much-celebrated Corvette ZR-1. McLellan, who retired from the company in 1992, is pictured here sitting in the 1,000,000th Corvette on the day it was made.

Corvette is the only sports car that has ever produced 1 million units. The box below gives year-by-year production numbers from 1953 through 1992:

YEAR	CONVERTIBLE	COUPE	TOTAL	YEAR	CONVERTIBLE	COUPE	TOTAL
1953	300		300	1973	4,943	25,521	30,464
1954	3,640		3,640	1974	5,474	32,028	37,502
1955	700	—	700	1975	4,629	33,836	38,465
1956	3,467		3,467	1976		46,558	46,558
1957	6,339		6,339	1977		49,213	49,213
1958	9,168		9,168	1978		46,776	46,776
1959	9,670		9,670	1979		53,807	53,807
1960	10,261		10,261	1980		40,614	40,614
1961	10,939		10,939	1981		40,606	40,606
1962	14,531		14,531	1982		25,407	25,407
1963	10,919	10,594	21,513	1983		*	*
1964	13,925	8,304	22,229	1984		51,547	51,547
1965	15,376	8,186	23,562	1985		39,729	39,729
1966	17,762	9,958	27,720	1986	7,315	27,794	35,109
1967	14,436	8,504	22,940	1987	10,625	20,007	30,632
1968	18,630	9,936	28,566	1988	7,407	15,382	22,789
1969	16,633	22,129	38,762	1989	9,749	16,663	26,412
1970	6,648	10,668	17,316	1990	7,630	16,016	23,646
1971	7,121	14,680	21,801	1991	5,672	14,967	20,639
1972	6,508	20,496	27,004	1992	5,514	14,143	**19,657
				TOTALS	**265,931**	**734,069**	**1,000,000**

* In 1983 there were a few cars produced for General Motors research and testing that were never sold.
** Through July 2, 1992

CHAPTER 8

THE 40ᵀᴴ YEAR EDITION: 1993

Corvettes are collector's cars. And because they are collectables, there have been many special edition Corvettes. Partly to celebrate 40 years of history, but mostly to meet the demand of the collectors (now and in the future), the 1993 models could be purchased with a special commemorative package called the "40th Year Edition."

It was an option package available on all models – coupe, convertible and ZR-1. All 40th Anniversary Edition Corvettes (and only 40th Anniversary Edition Corvettes) came in the color ruby red. They were ruby red, inside and out.

The car pictured here, most readers will agree, has a striking appearance. The effect in person is better described as "stunning." The deep-shining metallic exterior, with matching ruby red leather interior, came with emblems all over. The optional package price of $1,455 will, most likely, be worth many times that amount as the car ages and becomes a collector's prize.

Let's see, now, what should we expect in the year 2003? The golden anniversary model is probably not going to be red!

A 1993 Corvette with the 40th Anniversary package. These special edition cars came in only one color: ruby red.

Right: The 40th Anniversary logo. This package included an all ruby red interior with 40th Anniversary embroidery on the headrests; chrome-colored emblems on the hood, fuel door and side gills; a ruby red wheel hub insert; and the exclusive ruby red exterior paint.

The 40th Anniversary package was available on the standard Corvette, the Corvette convertible or the ZR-1. The convertible came with a ruby red soft top.

CHAPTER 9

CORVETTE IN AMERICA: CAR SHOWS

Corvette is more than just a car. It is a part of the owner's personality, value system and psychological make-up. The degree to which people are affected by "Corvette Fever" seems extraordinary. Visible evidence of this can be seen at any one of the hundreds of Corvette car shows held throughout the country each year. The two most famous of these are "Bloomington Gold" and "Corvettes at Carlisle."

Bloomington Gold gets its name from the location where the show was held for many years, Bloomington, Illinois. The show grew so large, in 1993 it had to be moved to the Illinois State Fairgrounds in Springfield. The word "gold" refers to the highest certificate given at the show's contests in factory originality (silver and bronze certificates are also awarded). A car that has received the Bloomington Gold certificate can be compared to a perfect, factory-original Corvette and is therefore very valuable. The show is held each year on the last weekend in June.

Corvettes at Carlisle is the largest Corvette car show each year. It is held in the small town of Carlisle, Pennsylvania, which is near Harrisburg. Typical events include the swap meet, vendor

The Bloomington Gold Certificate. Corvettes are judged by experts for their condition as compared to a factory-new car. Those that receive this award are 95 percent to 100 percent original quality.

An aerial shot of the "Corvettes at Carlisle" car show. In recent years, attendance has been over 30,000 people who come to ogle the more than 3,000 Corvettes.

The 1993 Carlisle "give away" car, a 1986 convertible with "Rick Mears Special Edition" package. Each year the car show holds a drawing for a Corvette.

display, drag racing, Corvette parade and the poster girl competition. Events that are special at Carlisle are the "give away" car (a drawing is held each year), the reunion of Callaway Corvettes (in 1992 there were 72 on display), and of course, the show's enormous size. Corvettes at Carlisle is held each year on the last weekend in August.

The "Road Tour" at Bloomington Gold. More than a thousand Corvettes line up for this annual parade, which lasts for hours.

CHAPTER 10

CORVETTE TODAY: LT1

Automotive writers the world over keep asking, "What country makes the best sports car?" In the 1990s, the answer may be "America."

At the heart of Corvette's success over the years has been its engine, and this is certainly true of the current models. Introduced in the 1992 model year, the LT1 5.7 liter V-8 replaced the L98 5.7 liter V-8 engine used on the Corvette since the 1985 model year. This second-generation Chevy small-block delivers 300 hp at 5000 rpm – the highest net horsepower from a production-car small-block in Chevy history – 50 hp more than the L98 engine it replaced.

The 1993 coupe and convertible come with a 4-speed automatic shift with lock up torque converter. A ZF manual 6-speed is available as a no-cost option. The 6-speed manual transmission was designed specifically for the Corvette by Zahradfabrik Friedshafen (ZF), a German transmission builder known worldwide for its gearboxes.

The 1993 Chevrolet Corvette Coupe. At the heart of this car's success is its small-block V-8, the LT1 engine. Similar to its namesake, the LT-1 first introduced in 1955, this engine is modeled after the power plant that powered more cars than any other V-8.

CORVETTE

Model	1993 LT1 Coupe
Engine	350ci (5.7 liter) V-8
Horsepower	300 hp @ 5000 rpm
Torque	340 lb-ft @ 3600 rpm
Gearbox	ZF 6-speed manual or 4-speed automatic
Maximum speed	163 mph
Acceleration	
0-60 mph	5.3 seconds
Standing	
quarter-mile	13.9 seconds @ 102 mph
Base price	$34,595 (coupe), $41,195 (convertible)

New technology has been a Corvette hallmark since the 1953 model introduced its plastic body. The 1993 car offers the new GM Passive Keyless Entry (PKE) system as standard equipment. Unlike other keyless entry systems that require the push of a button on a key-fob, the Corvette PKE requires no action – simply approach the car and the system automatically unlocks a door (or both doors, depending on the setting) and turns on the interior light. Walk away from the car and, within a few feet, the system automatically locks both doors. The PKE also automatically arms or disarms the Corvette theft-deterrent system.

Front and back shots of Corvette's 1993 convertible. Manufacturer's suggested retail price (MSRP) is $6,000 more than the coupe.

CHAPTER 11

CORVETTE TODAY: ZR-1

America's performance leader, the *car the motor press calls "King of the Hill," a 1993 Chevrolet Corvette ZR-1.*

Ever since it captured the lead on the sports car stage in 1990, the Corvette ZR-1 has been the headline grabber. It put an American sports car in league with the fastest Porsches, Ferraris and Lamborghinis.

For 1993, the Corvette ZR-1 came on even stronger. Its LT5 V-8, which is exclusive to the ZR-1, jumped 30 horsepower to 405 at 5800 rpm. Torque also increased to 385 lb-ft at 5200 rpm. This is information that is sure to make news in places like Stuttgart, Maranello and St. Agata.

Indy-class racing cars have a center of gravity (COG) that averages about 12 inches above the road. The ZR-1's COG is only 15 inches. It may make car entry a bit more difficult, but it is well worth it for the performance. Cornering and handling are determined by a car's suspension system, weight distribution and center of gravity. Corvette excels in all these areas.

If you can't look under the hood, how does one tell a $65,000 ZR-1 from the standard Corvette that is priced at about half as much ($35,000)? First, there is the small nameplate, "ZR-1," placed on each side and on the back. However, if you miss it or are too far away to read it, look for the slightly flared rear bodywork. It's a not-too-subtle sign of the extra-wide rear tires that are required to put LT5 power to the pavement.

In its 40-year history, Corvette has established a tradition of engineering leadership and innovation. The ZR-1 is today's example of that legend. It comes only as a coupe; there is no convertible.

Model	1993 ZR-1 Coupe
Engine	350ci (5.7 liter) V-8 LT5
Horsepower	405 hp @ 5800 rpm
Torque	385 lb-ft @ 5200 rpm
Gearbox	ZF 6-speed manual
Maximum speed	175 mph
Acceleration 0-60 mph	4.3 seconds
Standing quarter-mile	12.9 seconds @ 112 mph
Base price	$66,278

CHAPTER 12

AFTERMARKET: CALLAWAY CORVETTE

Chip Miller (left), director of Corvettes at Carlisle car show, and Reeves Callaway (right) with a new Callaway Speedster Corvette in the downtown Carlisle Parade.

The term "aftermarket" refers to work done on a car by others "after" it has left the manufacturer. The leading aftermarket work on the Corvette has been done by Reeves Callaway and his small company located in Old Lyme, Connecticut. Since the mid-'80s, Callaway Cars, Inc., has upgraded over 500 Corvettes. There is such great interest in these cars that some car shows, like Corvettes at Carlisle, hold special reunions for the aftermarket cars.

One of the most famous of the Callaway Corvettes was a 1988 model that Reeves Callaway named "the Sledgehammer." It is pictured here and the specifications are given in the box on the next page. Its top speed of 254.76 mph has been widely acclaimed by motor magazines as the fastest road car in the world. In talking with Corvette engineer Dave McLellan, Reeves Callaway was discussing the car and the fact that it was to be featured in a German car magazine with the cover line, "Das Is Der Hammer." (In German, the word "hammer" is slang for significant power.) McLellan joked to Callaway, "Das Is Der Sledgehammer!" The name has been used ever since.

Model	Callaway Corvette "Sledghammer"
Engine	Twin-turbocharged V-8 350ci (5.7 liter)
Horsepower	880 hp @ 6250 rpm
Torque	772 lb-ft @ 5250 rpm
Gearbox	ZF 6-speed manual
Maximum speed	254.76 mph
Acceleration 0-60 mph	3.9 seconds
Standing quarter-mile	10.6 seconds @ 146 mph

Just your average, run-of-the-mill, drive-to-the-grocery-store Callaway Corvette. If you're in a hurry this one will do 0-60 mph in 3.9 seconds and has a top speed of 254.76 mph. Callaway called this model the "Sledgehammer."

The most widely performed Corvette conversion has probably been the "Callaway Twin Turbo." However, this package has been discontinued, and Callaway now offers a new conversion called the "Callaway Speedster." It is available only on the ZR-1 Corvette.

The end of the line for the most widely ordered Corvette conversion. Pictured here is the last of the Callaway Twin Turbos. It was a birthday gift to Corvette collector Chip Miller in October, 1992. Miller owns 18 other Corvettes!

CHAPTER 13

CORVETTE TRIVIA QUIZ

Corvettes over the years. Can you identify which is the 1953, 1963, 1973 or 1993 model? Why didn't they include a 1983 model in this picture?

Here are ten questions to test your savvy about Corvettes and their history. The answers are on the next page.

1. In what year was the first Corvette made?
2. Did the first Corvette engines have 6, 8 or 12 cylinders?
3. What was the most famous "Fuelie" Corvette?
4. When was the convertible Corvette made?
5. When was the hardtop (coupe) Corvette made?
6. What is a "split rear window" Corvette?
7. Which is the correct spelling: "Sting Ray" or "Stingray"?
8. When was the first "big-block" engine introduced?
9. What was unusual about the 1983 model Corvette?
10. What year was the ZR-1 Corvette introduced?

How did you do? Using the answers given on the next page, score yourself according the following scale:

The current Corvette logo.

CORVETTE EXPERT:
9 or 10 correct answers
KNOWLEDGEABLE ABOUT CORVETTES:
7 or 8 correct answers
PERSON WHO CAN TALK ABOUT CORVETTES:
5 or 6 correct answers
PERSON WHO CAN LISTEN TO CORVETTE TALK:
3 or 4 correct answers
PERSON WHO NEEDS TO READ THIS BOOK:
0, 1 or 2 correct answers

Answers to the Corvette Trivia Quiz on page 29.

Many people think the mid-year 'Vettes, 1963 to 1967, are the most perfectly designed cars. This is a 1965 convertible.

NO FAIR PEEKING!

1. The first Corvettes were manufactured in 1953. Only 300 were made that year and they have become highly prized as collector's items.

2. The first Corvette engine was called the "Blue Flame Six." It was a 6-cylinder in-line motor rated at 150 horsepower.

3. The 1957 Corvette was the first to come with fuel injection system. Today the "'57 Fuelie" is a legend and famous for its racing victories.

4. Corvette started as a "convertible only" automobile in 1953 and was made every year until 1975. The convertible was started again in 1986 and is still being made today.

5. The first Corvette coupe was offered in 1963 and has been made every year since.

6. The first Corvette coupe ('63) came with a two-piece rear window. The next year the window was redesigned and has, since then, always been a single piece of glass.

7. Trick question. Both spellings are correct. The original "Sting Ray" was made from 1963 to 1967. In 1968 the term was not used. In 1969 the name was reintroduced and spelled as one word, "Stingray," until it was discontinued the second time in 1976.

8. The first "big-block" was introduced in 1965. Large displacement engines of 396, 427 and 454 cubic inches, were available from 1965 through 1974.

9. There was no 1983 model Corvette.

10. The ZR-1 was introduced in 1990 and is still being offered as this book is written.

29

CHAPTER 14

CORVETTE: IMPORTANT DATES

1953 First public showing of the Corvette, January, 1953, at the GM Motorama car show in New York City. By June the Corvette was in production at a temporary facility in Flint, Michigan, where 300 Corvettes were made that year.

1954 Corvette production moved to a renovated facility in St. Louis, Missouri. Chevrolet built 3,640 of the 1954 models. Approximately 1,100 remained unsold at year's end.

1955 Next to 1953, this was the lowest volume Corvette. Only 700 1955 models were built. Many writers predicted this would be the last year and production would be dropped.

1957 A milestone in the history of the American motor car, the 1957 Corvette was the first to combine fuel-injection with a 4-speed manual transmission. Two important racing wins were Sebring and the SCCA National Title. Sales jumped to 6,339.

1958 The first Corvette with four headlights and factory-installed seat belts. Corvettes were unchallenged in SCCA racing. Sales increased again to 9,168.

1962 This was the last Corvette with conventional trunk and the last with a solid rear axle. Sales increased to 14,531.

1963 New body style, called "Sting Ray," was introduced. Available both as a fastback coupe and convertible for the first time. Called the "best-handling sports car in the world," sales went through the roof and totaled 21,513.

1965 Big-block engines were introduced. The RPO L78 had 396ci and 425 hp. The Sting Ray was changed from a well-balanced sports car into a tire-shredding, sideways-driving monster.

1967 Last of the 1963-67 "mid-year" Corvettes, the '67 model is now called the "best Sting Ray, ever." The big L88 exceeded 500 hp and could do 0-60 in 5.5 seconds and the quarter-mile in 13.8 seconds at 104 mph. This left the Shelby-Cobra in second place with 0-60 of 6.2 seconds and the quarter-mile in 14.5 seconds at 101 mph.

1968 The all new Mako Shark body was introduced and the name Sting Ray dropped. Production increased to 28,566.

1969 The name "Stingray" reappeared as one word and remained through 1976. Production totaled 38,762, a level not reached again until 1976.

1971 Called "the last of the fast ones," 1971 marked the end of the screaming big-blocks. Many thought '71 was the swan song of Corvette high performance, and this would be the last Corvette worth owning. Production was 21,801.

1976 The convertible was gone, but that didn't stop 46,558 people from purchasing new 1976 Corvettes.

1978 The "25th Anniversary" year offered silver paint schemes and "replicas" of the 1978 Indianapolis 500 Pace Car. The window sticker of $13,653 was sometimes doubled as a street price. Sales were 46,776 including 6,502 pace car replicas.

1981 This was the year of transition for Corvette, as the new assembly plant in Bowling Green, Kentucky started production.

1982 This model was the end of the body series that began in 1968 and the chassis design that started in 1963. At $22,537.59, the '82 Collector Edition (only) was the first Corvette to sell above the $20,000 mark. Cross-fire injection was introduced.

1983 There was no '83 Corvette.

1984 The all-new '84 model was introduced in March, 1983 and was a radical departure from anything Chevrolet had ever built. Performance was less than the '60s, but good enough to do 0-60 in less than 7 seconds and have a top speed of more than 140 mph.

1986 A good example of why you should "never say never": after publicizing the '75 model as the "last" convertible, Corvette reintroduced the ragtop in 1986 and has made one every year since. Production of 35,109 included 7,315 convertibles.

1992 Corvette builds its 1,000,000th car.

GLOSSARY

ABS – Anti-lock Braking System. Sensors monitor wheel rotation and prevent wheel lockup during braking by modulating hydraulic pressure.

Big-Block – Large displacement engines of 396, 427 and 454 cubic inches, optional in Corvettes from 1965 through 1974.

Bloomington – The popular annual Corvette show known for its certification judging system based on factory originality. Held in Bloomington, Illinois 1973-92, then in Springfield, Illinois since 1993.

ci – Cubic inches. Refers to the amount of space in the engine cylinders. The larger the number, the larger the engine and power.

Callaway – Engine conversion, often called "Callaway Twin Turbo," by Callaway Engineering, Old Lyme, Connecticut. Available through Chevrolet dealers since 1987.

Classic – Corvette models 1953 through 1962.

Duntov – Zora Arkus-Duntov, legendary chief engineer, called "father" of the Corvette. Also, the highest award of the National Corvette Restorers Society (NCRS).

Fuelie – The fuel-injected Corvettes of 1957 through 1965.

Gold Certificate – Top Bloomington award for factory originality.

Knock-Off – Cast aluminum wheel option for 1963 through 1966 models.

Mid-Year – Corvette models 1963 through 1967.

mph – Miles per hour. The speed of a car in miles per hour.

Sting Ray – 1963 through 1967 Corvette.

Stingray – 1969 through 1976 Corvette.

ZR-1 – Corvette model introduced in 1990 with special 32-valve overhead cam engine. Also, the 1970 through 1972 engine option (ZR1).

INDEX